KIRKIE MORRISSEY

THE

Responsive Heart

A Bible Study for Women Based on the Parable of the Sower

CULTIVATING A LIFE-LONG LOVE FOR GOD

NavPress

Bringing Truth to Life

P.O. Box 35001, Colorado Springs, Colorado 80935

OUR GUARANTEE TO YOU

We believe so strongly in the message of our books that we are making this quality guarantee to you. If for any reason you are disappointed with the content of this book, return the title page to us with your name and address and we will refund to you the list price of the book. To help us serve you better, please briefly describe why you were disappointed. Mail your refund request to: NavPress, P.O. Box 35002, Colorado Springs, CO 80935.

The Navigators is an international Christian organization. Our mission is to reach, disciple, and equip people to know Christ and to make Him known through successive generations. We envision multitudes of diverse people in the United States and every other nation who have a passionate love for Christ, live a lifestyle of sharing Christ's love, and multiply spiritual laborers among those without Christ.

NavPress is the publishing ministry of The Navigators. NavPress publications help believers learn biblical truth and apply what they learn to their lives and ministries. Our mission is to stimulate spiritual formation among our readers.

ISBN 1-57683-181-7

Cover design by Ray Moore
Cover photo by Ryann Cooley

All Scripture quotations in this publication are taken from the *HOLY BIBLE: NEW INTERNATIONAL VERSION* ® (NIV®), copyright © 1973, 1978, 1984 by International Bible Society. Used by permission of Zondervan Publishing House. All rights reserved.

Printed in the United States of America

1 2 3 4 5 6 7 8 9 10 11 12 13 14 15 / 05 04 03 02 01 00

Contents

Acknowledgments

Dedicated to my dear friend Ann
with appreciation for years of
editing study drafts,
but most of all,
for her faithful friendship,
prayer support, and caring ways.
I give thanks for her love for the Lord
and her servant heart,
which have touched my heart and blessed my life.
In addition, the witness of her life
has impacted many
and daily brings glory to God.

My appreciation is also extended to the staff at First Presbyterian Church for providing me with opportunities to teach. I especially thank Kathy Boyles, director of Women's Ministries, who requested that I teach a weekly class for women called Women ALIVE! during the school year. Writing the material and teaching this class have provided the springboard for these studies now published by NavPress. I am also thankful to the women in that class for their prayers, encouragement, and friendship.

In addition, I am very grateful to the staff at NavPress. Special thanks are extended to Paul Santhouse for his support, to Terri Hibbard for her work editing all the material initially included in this study, and to Terry Behimer, project coordinator. NavPress has been so nice to work with, and I appreciate their gracious support and encouragement.

Introduction

Do you enjoy a beautiful garden? Have you created one of your own, or do you appreciate those created by others? Many communities feature gardens that are major attractions. For example, Denver has its renowned Botanical Gardens that are delightful to view. Whether for public attraction or private enjoyment, we are aware that it takes more than just desire or good intentions to produce a flowering wonderland. And so it is with the garden of our hearts. Just as a garden responds and produces abundantly under the loving, nurturing care of a master gardener, so will our lives flourish and produce an abundance of results as we respond to the love of the Lord, our Master Gardener.

For flowering plants, trees, and vegetation to flourish, a combination of rich soil, sun, water, and healthy root systems are also essential. Evidence of this is seen clearly throughout nature. When any of these important elements are missing, the health of the plant is compromised.

Every gardener knows that different types of plants need different *types* of soil, but all plants need *good* soil. Without it, they will die or produce only poor flowers, fruits, or vegetables. If either sun or water is removed, plants will not survive. And without strong, deep roots, even trees are easily toppled in strong winds. Consider the hurricane season in Florida. Being at sea level means there is little depth of soil, which prevents trees from growing deep roots. Without deep roots, the trees are without defense during severe storms and many are easily toppled.

How does all of this relate to our spiritual growth? There are many parallels that Jesus uses in His Parable of the Sower (recorded in Matthew 13, Mark 4, and Luke 8). Here He reveals what is necessary to live productively, as well as how to overcome all that threatens the growth of our faith. This knowledge enables us to withstand the storms of life. In fact, we discover that storms may not necessarily harm us, but can strengthen us in our faith! Just as a tree on a ridge becomes stronger when exposed to gusty winds, so we in our faith can deepen our roots in Christ through trials that come our way. Not only are we strengthened, but as we grow in the Lord, our lives become increasingly productive and our joy in Him abounds.

We will examine Jesus' warnings, instructions, and promises. Because He is the creator and sustainer of life, it is essential for us to heed His words. God the Father underscores this when, on the Mount of Transfiguration, His voice echoes urgently and compassionately: "This is my Son . . . Listen to him!" (Matthew 17:5). As we listen, a "responsive heart" is nurtured within us. Some results of a responsive heart can be that we know Him better, our love for Him deepens, our peace increases, our lives become more productive, and our joy heightens.

> "Now I commit you to God and to the word of his grace, which can build you up and give you an inheritance among all those who are sanctified."
> —Acts 20:32

CHAPTER ONE

Receiving the Seed

"The knowledge of the secrets of the kingdom of heaven has been given to you."

—Matthew 13:11

"I have told you this so that my joy may be in you and that your joy may be complete."

—John 15:11

God is a communicator! In the beginning He walked and talked face to face with Adam and Eve. Out of His heart of love and His longing for people to know Him, He then spoke for many years through the prophets and provided the Scriptures through which He still speaks today. Out of His deep desire that we would know Him more completely and understand His love more fully, God Himself then came to earth in the person of Jesus Christ. In addition to revealing Himself, an important part of Jesus' mission was to instruct those who would listen to His teachings about the essentials of life.

To do so, Jesus often taught in parables. Using imagery and scenarios common to everyday life, He generally imparted one main truth in each parable. For those who truly desired understanding, Jesus carefully explained His message in detail.

In this chapter we will do an overview of the Parable of the Sower and related themes, including examining the soil, receiving the seed, understanding the importance of strong, deep roots, and obeying what God has revealed. Jesus' desire in teaching us these truths is that we would know Him and have "life, and have it to the full" (John 10:10).

Examination of God's Word

In His Parable of the Sower, Jesus gives critical insight into how our spirits receive true life. Physical life begins with a seed. This is true of plant life, animal life, and human life. Likewise, spiritual life comes from the seed God plants in the human heart. Because God knows a life of faith is challenging in this world of competition and opposition, He carefully reveals all we need not only to survive, but to flourish.

To examine His words of instruction and warning, turn to Matthew 13:1-9,18-23, and answer the questions that follow.

1. Complete the chart below, which provides an overview of this study.

Verses	Type of Soil	Result	Reason
4,19			
5-6,20-21			
7,22			
8,23			

2. What do you think Jesus' primary message is in this parable? What speaks to you initially from this parable?

8

3.   What instruction does Jesus give you?

4.   What warnings does He issue?

5.   Read Matthew 17:5 and John 14:6. Based on these verses, why is it important to heed what Jesus has to say?

Referring to the Parable of the Sower as recorded in Matthew 13, Mark 4, and Luke 8, U.S. Senate chaplin and author Dr. Lloyd John Ogilvie states, "Considered together, the three versions stress that a hearing heart receives, responds, reproduces, and is relentless."[1]

6.   When you hear or read God's truths, how do you usually respond? Check one of the following options.

   ☐ I find them interesting, but quickly move on to more pressing issues, feeling I've fulfilled my spiritual duty for the day.
   ☐ I find them interesting and would like to spend more time reflecting on them, but feel pushed with demands, so I move on reluctantly to the next item on the schedule.
   ☐ I find them difficult to believe, so I more or less write them off.
   ☐ I find them difficult to believe for me, believing they are true for others who are perhaps more visible in the faith.
   ☐ I find them satisfying as I take time to meditate on the truths; I ask questions and seek insight regarding them; I reflect on them at various times throughout the day; and I respond, desiring to incorporate them into my life.
   ☐ Other:

The impact of Jesus' teaching is always enhanced for me when I personally witness an example in nature. As we have moved from one location to another, we have experienced a variety of soil compositions. For a while we lived in an area in Colorado Springs where the ground was very rocky and the soil was like hardened clay. It was virtually impossible to grow anything there. In contrast, our previous home had rich, good soil. It came with a wonderful garden that had been lovingly cared for and was producing vegetables and flowers in abundance. We thoroughly enjoyed and delighted in it. Due to the differences in the soil at these two homes, the potential for crops varied. These experiences, and others like them, help me understand what Jesus was illustrating in this familiar parable.

7. What truths from this parable have you seen evidenced in nature? What impact do these experiences have on your understanding of the spiritual truths of Matthew 13?

8. Who is the farmer in Jesus' parable? (See also Matthew 13:37 in Jesus' explanation of the weeds.)

9. According to verses 18-19, what is the seed?

10. How does Jesus illustrate this parable in Matthew 4:23?

11. What was God's "heart reason" for sending Jesus, according to John 3:16?

12. Based on John 1:1-4 and Mark 1:14-15, what is the relationship between Jesus, the seed, and God's Word?

According to the *New International Dictionary of the Bible,* "the word of God is the fundamental aspect of God's self-revelation, for by his word he makes known who he is, what he is like, and what his will is for the world."[2] Therefore, when Christ is described as the Word, it is another way of underscoring that Jesus is God, revealing to us what God is like and what He has planned for us.

13. In the Parable of the Sower, what was identified as the good soil? (See Matthew 13:18-23.)

14. What insight does the truth that Jesus is the Word give you concerning this parable?

15. Read John 1:11-12. What key word or concept is used in both verses? Why is this action so important?

16. In what ways is the condition of the soil related to a plant's ability to receive the seed and grow deep roots? How does this compare with the condition of our hearts and our ability to respond to the things of God?

17. What are some functions of the roots of physical plants? How do they compare to the importance of being rooted in Christ as mentioned in Colossians 2:6-7?

The deeper the roots, the heartier a plant or tree will become. By being firmly established in the soil, it survives difficult conditions and even bears fruit during such times. Jeremiah applies this truth spiritually by saying:

> Blessed is the man who trusts in the LORD,
>   whose confidence is in him.
> He will be like a tree planted by the water
>   that sends out its roots by the stream.
> It does not fear when heat comes;
>   its leaves are always green.
> It has no worries in a year of drought
>   and never fails to bear fruit. (Jeremiah 17:7-8)

18. A danger to preventing roots from growing deeper is expressed in Hebrews 5:11–6:1. What observation does the writer make concerning the importance of spiritual growth?

In his book *The Inner Life*, Andrew Murray addresses another common hindrance that prevents the growth of spiritual roots. He differentiates between simply knowing truths in our heads and getting them to root in our hearts.

The one great lesson the Spirit seeks to enforce in regard to God's Word is this: Only as Scripture is received out of the life of God into our life can there be any real knowledge of it. The Word is a seed that bears within it the divine life. When it is received in the good soil of a heart that hungers for that life, it will spring up and bring forth fruit like all seed, "after its kind." It will reproduce in our life the very life of God. . . . The Word of God must be received into the life and not only in the mind.[3]

19.   Why do truths need to root in our hearts as well as our minds?

20.   In Luke 8:8, what does Jesus say He desires the result to be of this seed rooting in good soil?

21.   What else is necessary to grow deeper in the Lord, according to Philippians 3:16?

22.   What principle from God's economy does Jesus share in Matthew 13:11-12?

Oswald Chambers sees a relationship between being obedient to what God has already said before expecting Him to reveal more of His will. He writes, "All of God's revealed truths are sealed until they are opened to us through obedience. . . . God will never reveal more truth about Himself to you until you have obeyed what you know already."[4]

23.   Why do you think God places this stipulation upon us for growing deeper in Him?

Reflection and Application

24.   Reflecting on this parable, how would you describe the soil of your heart or life right now? How is the condition of the soil evidenced in your life?

25.   Have you received the seed of Christ's life in your heart? If not, would you like to respond now? Jesus promises, "Ask and it will be given to you" (Luke 11:9-10).

Between You and God

26.   What personal distractions sidetrack you from growing in Christ? For each one you think of, jot down some ideas of how to eliminate or deal with it.

Faith is like a spiritual muscle—when it is used, it becomes strengthened. Roots grow deeper in the Lord when we act on what we know to be true. As we find Him to be all He claims to be, we're encouraged to continue further and deeper.

27.   To what situation in your life right now can you apply God's revealed truth in a new way? Record it here (or in your journal), along with the truths you will depend upon.

CHAPTER TWO

Removing Rocks and Weeds

"The one who received the seed that fell on rocky places is the man who hears the word and at once receives it with joy. But since he has no root, he lasts only a short time."

—Matthew 13:20-21

"Since we are surrounded by such a great cloud of witnesses, let us throw off everything that hinders and the sin that so easily entangles."

—Hebrews 12:1

Have you ever visited the Rocky Mountains? If so, you probably noticed that as the terrain gets rockier, the plants get fewer and smaller. Generally, rocky places have very little soil to support plant life. If anything does take root, it is very difficult for life to be sustained. It is not uncommon to see saplings or plants lying withered and dried in the rockier places.

Every gardener knows that it is important to examine carefully the condition of the soil before investing time, money, and energy in planting a garden. Farmers know they must clear their fields of rocks before they can plow and sow their crops. If they fail to do so, crops will not flourish.

These same principles apply to nurturing the spiritual seed sown in our lives. To explore these parallels, turn once again to the Parable of the Sower in Matthew 13:3-9, 18-23.

Examination of God's Word

The *World Book Encyclopedia* advises, "In preparing the soil, first remove any large stones or rubbish from the garden site. If grass or other plants [weeds] cover the site, use a spade or shovel to dig under the roots of the plants and remove them."[1] This obvious principle is often overlooked in our spiritual lives.

1. What happens to the seed sown in the rocky places to which Jesus refers in Matthew 13:5?

2. a. What are the characteristics of rocky soil that thwart the growth of plant life?

   b. What are the characteristics of good soil that promote life?

3. In what ways do these same characteristics pertain to our hearts?

4. How does the warning given to us in Hebrews 3:12-13 apply to this parable?

5. Just as a physical garden is negatively impacted by rocks and weeds, the spiritual garden of one's heart is hindered by many things. What might these rocks and weeds symbolize in our hearts and lives?

Like a gardener or farmer, we each have a choice regarding the condition of our heart's soil and the harvest of our life's garden. Often we pay closer attention to caring for our fruit or vegetable gardens than to nurturing our lives. For a warning and an encouragement about spiritual gardening principles, read Galatians 6:7-9.

6.   Write the warning below in your own words.

7.   What personal encouragement do you receive from these verses?

8.   The *World Book* writer adds, "Not only do weeds shelter pests, but weeds also take food, water, and space from garden plants."[2] Why would it be important to remove weeds, rocks, and rubbish from the soil of your heart if you desire to sow "to please the Spirit"?

9.   What tool does the Lord use to uncover the weeds, rocks, and rubbish identified in Hebrews 4:12-13?

10.   In Colossians 3:5-10, the apostle Paul gives insight into what cleaning up the soil of our lives means. What does he specifically tell us to get rid of?

When the Holy Spirit reveals these or other rocks and weeds, a normal response is guilt. Probably none of us likes feeling guilty because it's uncomfortable. Most of us need affirmation, not condemnation. We want to feel good about ourselves, not criticized. Yet, just as a loving parent corrects a child for his or her own good, there is a place for our heavenly Father's correction as well.

11. When God makes us aware of what is not right in our lives, is it to condemn us? Review John 3:16-17 and Hebrews 12:10-11 for insight into this issue.

BETWEEN YOU AND ME

Guilt can be good. It's like the physical symptom that lets one know something is wrong with his or her health. Some time ago I had a mark on my face that I didn't pay much attention to. During a routine office visit, an observant doctor recognized immediately that this seemingly innocent spot was a symptom of an insidious cancer that had spread beneath the skin's surface. While I was ignoring the outward manifestation, the cancer had the potential to destroy me. Identifying the problem led to the prompt surgical removal of it.

Guilt can be such a symptom spiritually. God, the Great Physician, recognizes that something within us is destroying us. Therefore, in His love, He alerts us to it and advises that it be removed. Yet He performs this surgery only with our consent.

12. Read Psalm 32:1-5 and 1 John 1:9 for a biblical perspective of sin and guilt. Based on these verses, how can we be free from spiritual rocks and weeds?

When we are weeding, we can see only the tops of weeds above the soil. Obviously it is ineffective to just snip off the visible part of these nuisances. Without removing the roots, the weeds will continue to grow. In our spiritual gardens we often deal with only the visible portion of sin.

13. What might be the root sin of each of the observable sins (weeds) listed below?

Observable sin:	_Possible root sin:_
•Saying something hurtful to another	•
•Losing one's temper	•
•Spreading gossip	•
•Not telling the truth	•
•Taking credit belonging to another	•
•Showing favoritism	•
•Not doing something the Lord asks	•
• Not seeking God's direction	•

14. Read Matthew 6:14-15 and identify a common root that is often difficult to deal with.

15. Why is this one so hard to get rid of?

16. What are reasons why people may not want to forgive?

17. According to Ephesians 4:30-32, in what manner are we exhorted to forgive?

18. The writer of Hebrews is very direct about how to handle things that hinder our growth. What are we commanded to do in Hebrews 12:1-2?

19. God understands our struggles with sin. According to Hebrews 4:15-16, what help is available to us in Him?

20. Some reasons people do not cast off sin are lack of knowledge, lack of power, and lack of desire. Through the Holy Spirit, God enables us to deal with all three reasons. Look up each of the Scriptures listed below and record your findings.

   a. Lack of knowledge—Proverbs 20:27; John 14:16-17; Ephesians 5:13-14

   b. Lack of power—Luke 10:19; Hebrews 2:17-18; 1 John 4:4

   c. Lack of desire—Philippians 2:13; James 4:1-2

21.   In John 12:42-43 and 1 Thessalonians 2:4-6, we see another obstacle to growing deep roots in Christ. Write this hindrance in your own words.

22.   Why do you think the praise of others becomes so important to us? How can we overcome this so that God's praise is all that matters?

In nature, some threats to crops appear less menacing than others. In early spring baby rabbits are cute to watch, but any gardener knows they can wreak havoc on new sprouts. Likewise, Solomon names another "cute" destroyer of crops in Song of Songs 2:15.

23.   What does Solomon say we are to do with such critters?

24.   How does this truth apply to our spiritual lives? In light of your discoveries in this study so far, what does this involve?

Reflection and Application
25.   Review questions 5, 8, 11, 12, 18, and 19. Write down any rocks or weeds you recognize in your own life.

26. In nurturing a responsive heart, seek God's help in dealing with these things. As He leads you, use a separate sheet of paper on which to write specific sins you want to confess. As you confess each one, cross it off your list. Afterward, take the paper and either burn it or shred it and throw it in the trash. A responsive heart is a cleansed heart, and the result is peace!

BETWEEN YOU AND ME

When I was in college I had a friendship with a young man that I knew was not the best for me. The Lord convicted me of this and directed me to break it off. I kept praying for the strength to do so, but never seemed to receive it. Then the Lord revealed to me my root problem: I really didn't want to end it. I was enjoying the relationship and wanted to hang on to it. The Lord showed me I had to start where I was. First, I had to confess not really wanting to obey and therefore not wanting His help. Then I had to ask Him to help me truly want to be obedient and to "want to want" His strength to do what I knew was right to do. As I began where I was, He then could meet me in it. He forgave me, then enabled me truly to desire His help in being obedient. As my heart was changed, He gave me the strength I needed to terminate the relationship. The result was joy in Him and peace within.

27. Read Psalm 103:11-12 and write these verses in your own words below. Personalize them and rest in their truth.

28. Ask the Lord to show you if you have dealt with the visible sins (or symptoms) or the roots (heart problems) in your life. As roots are revealed, confess them, asking Him to remove each. Whenever one resurfaces, repeat this process until the weed is totally removed.

Between You and God

When we focus on ourselves, our wants and pleasures, we are not seeing the total picture. We need God's perspective—an eternal perspective. As we search the Scriptures for God's desires and understand why they are best, those become our heart's desires as well. We then cry out to God as David did, "Search me, O God, and know my heart; test me and know my anxious thoughts. See if there is any offensive way in me, and lead me in the way everlasting" (Psalm 139:23-24). Heinrich Suso, a Dominican friar of the fourteenth century, wrote a dialogue in which Eternal Wisdom reveals: "If he knew that my glory depended on rooting out nettles or other weeds, that would be to him the most desirable thing to accomplish."[3]

29. Specifically ask God to reveal to you anyone you have not for-given or anyone against whom you are holding anger or bitter-ness in your heart. Write the name(s) here.

On the basis of Hebrews 4:15-16, be assured that God understands your hurt and your heart. Spend some time talking with Him about any struggles you have in this area. Ask Him to heal you of the hurts and to enable you to forgive by His Spirit within you.

30. Express your heart to the Lord in this way below. If you feel unable to forgive, tell Him that. Then ask Him to help you "want to want" His help.

Read John 8:31 and Ephesians 4:30. Ask God for His strength in your specific areas of weakness.

CHAPTER THREE

Cultivating Good Soil

"Still other seed fell on good soil, where it produced a crop – a hundred, sixty or thirty times what was sown. . . . But the one who received the seed that fell on good soil is the man who hears the word and understands it."

—Matthew 13:8,23

"You did not choose me, but I chose you and appointed you to go and bear fruit."

—John 15:16

Not only does the Lord desire for us to have a productive life that has eternal value, He *calls* us to this! As our hearts are responsive to His call, we discover there are two aspects involved: what we do, and who we are.

In his book *Gardens of the Heart*, Leroy Brownlow extols the benefits of such cultivation: "Within each of us lies a garden of the heart—a place where God can plant, water, cultivate, and gently nurture a beautiful harvest of character. But it is not just any harvest. . . . Yes, He plants and waters the fruit of the Spirit. . . . As we allow our hearts and minds to become God's garden, we shall find that we will be blessed beyond all expectation. Our lives will become filled with His qualities, His attributes. The garden will become like the Gardener. And that is God's greatest desire—for us to become like Him."[1]

In the previous chapter we explored the importance of removing unwanted attitudes and actions. Now let us examine what "good soil" is and pursue how to enrich the soil in our hearts, cultivating it to become more responsive to our Lord.

Examination of God's Word

1. According to Jesus' Parable of the Sower, what are the results of sowing seed in good soil? (See Matthew 13:8.) In your own words explain what this means.

2. Read John 15:8, 16. What is God's will and expectation about the fruit of our lives?

3. In Colossians 3, after Paul instructs us specifically in what to remove, he goes on to explain what beneficial nutrients we are to add. What are Paul's directives in Colossians 3:12-17?

    Knowing *what* to add is one thing. Knowing *how* to do so is another.

4. According to John 17:17 and 2 Timothy 3:15-17, what is one avenue through which spiritual nutrients are cultivated into our lives?

5. What specific works are accomplished through this means?

In John 17:17 above we read that Jesus prayed, "Sanctify them by your Word," and Paul states God's Word is helpful for "training in righteousness." Perhaps these terms and concepts are unfamiliar. Often it seems we hear a lot about being saved and little about becoming sanctified. Sanctification is our growth in Christlikeness, being made holy by God's Spirit. Because of our position in Christ we have already been made righteous; yet, the Lord desires us to reflect this in increasing measure in our lives now. This is portrayed in Hebrews 10:14 in which the writer states, "By one sacrifice he has made perfect forever those who are being made holy."

In 2 Timothy 1:9 Paul writes, "[God] has saved us and called us to a holy life." Many receive their salvation in Christ and then stop there. When we do this, we miss out! More importantly, God is grieved and is not fully glorified. In fact, in addition to "holiness," inherent in our salvation is God's desire to impart "wholeness" to us. The root word of "salvation" in Latin is *salus*, which means "wholeness"!

The Lord works His righteousness in those with a responsive heart, and brings us increasingly into wholeness in Him. In addition, as Christ is manifested more fully, we experience true life, our peace deepens, our joy heightens, our lives are productive, and God is glorified!

6.   In addition to Jesus' claim about God's Word in John 17:17, what does Paul proclaim in Acts 20:32?

7.   In 1 Thessalonians 5:23-24, what does Paul pray and what does he promise? Would you like to make this your prayer as well?

8. Regardless of whether or not we are aware of the Lord meeting us through His Word or accomplishing a work in us, what *is* occurring at a deep level according to Paul in 1 Thessalonians 2:13?

It is important to consider the relationship between fact (God's Word), faith (our confidence in God), and feelings (our subjective response to God's Word).

BETWEEN YOU AND ME

Too often we operate on the premise that what we feel is what is truth! I find myself having to battle this. I have found the Enemy quick to use how I feel and how things look to attempt to discourage me and defeat me.

The only way to overcome letting feelings determine faith is to *base our faith upon the Word of God, which is truth.* Because it is truth we can trust it regardless of our feelings. Faith must be firmly established on *fact*—then feelings follow. Our focus shifts from us and our circumstances to God and His Word. Consequently, instead of discouragement we have hope, and instead of defeat we have victory! When I am tempted to let feelings determine faith, I immediately ask myself, "What is truth?" Then I establish my faith upon that.

The Lord provides an analogy for this in His name, the "Sun of Righteousness" (Malachi 4:2). On a cool, cloudy day we don't panic, crying that the sun is gone just because we cannot feel its warmth or see its light. We are confident that the sun is there based upon fact. We know the sun is established in the heavens and all revolves around it. In the same way Jesus wants us to be absolutely confident that He is there, whether or not we see His light or feel the warmth of His love. It is fact! He is firmly established! He is the living God and promises never to leave us or forsake us (Hebrews 13:5).

9. In addition to His Word, another avenue available to us to nurture a responsive heart and to cultivate good soil is revealed in Philippians 1:9-11 and 1 Thessalonians 5:16-18. What is it?

10. In your own words define prayer.

11. What do you think is the main reason people pray?

12. Read each Scripture passage listed below. What encouragement is given about the power of prayer?

    a. John 15:7

    b. Acts 4:31

    c. James 5:16

13. When spending time in prayer and communion with the Lord, what are we guaranteed according to Psalm 145:18 and James 4:8? Remember, this is fact. Truth! What are you to do if you doubt that He meets you as you come to Him?

14. What promises and conditions does God put on prayer? Read each of the verses listed and record your findings in the chart below.

Verse	Promise	Condition
Matthew 6:5-6		
Luke 11:9-13		
John 14:13		
James 1:5		
1 John 5:14-15		

15. What insight do you gain into why we can pray according to His will in 1 Corinthians 2:16?

It is difficult to overemphasize the importance of prayer or the consequences of a life without prayer. In his devotional book *My Utmost for His Highest*, Oswald Chambers points out that for the person who does not pray, "what will suffer is the life of the Son of God in him, which is nourished not by food, but by prayer."[2] Not only does God command us to pray, He also gives us examples of how to pray.

16. Read in Matthew 6:9-13 the prayer Jesus gave us and Philippians 1:9-11 for an example from Paul's life. Jot down any new insights you gain.

17. In addition to God's Word and prayer, read about another important dimension of cultivating good soil in Luke 11:34-36 and Philippians 4:8. Write down what you discover.

18. How does this relate to 2 Corinthians 10:5? What specifically does this involve?

19. What challenges or difficulties confront us regarding this in our world today?

20.   Another important way to produce good soil is illustrated by the apostles in Acts 2:42 and also identified specifically in Hebrews 10:25. What is this ingredient?

21.   According to 1 John 1:5-7, what must we personally do to receive the benefit of fellowship with other believers?

22.   Some specific aspects of fellowship are mentioned in Psalm 147. Record these below.

a. verse 1

b. verse 6

c. verse 7

d. verse 11

Personally, I have discovered that truly only one thing is needed—time spent cultivating my spiritual garden. Therefore I plan daily times of at least an hour and one extended time weekly to spend alone with the Lord. If, due to many other demands, I am tempted to drop a scheduled time, I remind myself, *This is the most important thing I have to do today.* To protect these times, I have found it helpful to write them on the calendar and to treat them as I would any other important meeting or appointment. When someone wants to get together during that time I respond very honestly, "I'm sorry. I already have a commitment. Can we arrange another time?" I place at least as much (if not more) importance on my meeting with the living Lord as I would if I were meeting a friend or business associate.

23. Read again the quote of Leroy Brownlow on page 25. According to this quote and 2 Corinthians 3:18, what happens to us as we spend personal time with the Lord?

24. Based on Galatians 5:22-23, as the seed of the Person of Christ is nurtured within us by His Spirit, what fruit grows in the garden of our lives (within our being)?

25. What would be the practical results of these qualities of Christ in you? In your relationships with others?

26. From the Song of Songs, what commendation does the Lover (representing the Lord) give His beloved (us) in 4:10-15? What would this mean to you to have the Lord delight in you like this?

To have the Lord delight in the *fruit of His life in us* (His qualities manifested in us) brings joy to us as well as to Him. Then, Jesus speaks of other results of our life that He longs to see as the *fruit of His life flowing through us.*

27. Read John 15:5, 16. According to these verses, what additional "fruit" does Jesus call us to bear? What does this mean?

28. When Jesus uses the analogy of the vine and the branches in John 15:4-5, what is He revealing that is essential to the bearing of this fruit?

Reflection and Application
We have seen that our spiritual gardens are nurtured by spending time in God's Word, prayer, and in fellowship with other believers. The combined result is conformity to Christ. Is this your heart's desire? If so, it is important to understand that this transformation is a process (2 Corinthians 3:18). Maturity in Christ takes consistent discipline over time. This begins with defining where you are right now and developing a plan to get you where you want to be. Use the following questions to help you evaluate your personal heart's desire, priorities, and use of time. Then complete the "Personal Evaluation" at the end of this chapter.

29.	What does Paul reveal to be the goal and end result of "being rooted and established" in the love of Christ, clearly stated in Ephesians 3:14-19?

30.	As you think about becoming increasingly filled with Christ, what thoughts do you have? Is this a desire of your heart? If not, why?

It is important to examine if, deep down, we really do not want the good soil of Christ's life in us to any great degree. Talk with the Lord honestly regarding your discoveries.

Journaling is a helpful tool in prayer. As we pour out the expressions of our heart to Him on paper, He gives insight into what is truly going on within us. In addition, as we are honest with Him, He is able to meet us effectively where we are. A journal also provides a helpful record of requests made, answers given, and growth accomplished.

If you have never kept a journal before, write as though you are simply talking with Jesus or writing a letter to Him. Share your feelings, your fears. Respond to glimpses you get as you write. Allow Him to meet you and guide you.

31.	Are you currently spending time daily with the Lord, studying and meditating upon His Word?

	▪ If so, when do you find is the best time for you?

	▪ If not, what keeps you from a daily time with God?

Between You and God

Use the following "Personal Evaluation" to determine how to align your heart's desire with God's Word in a practical way in your life. It may be helpful to review your responses throughout this chapter as you complete the worksheet.

PERSONAL EVALUATION

My Heart's Desire
- I want to be known as a person who:

- My ultimate goal or passion is to:

Reflection: What do these responses reflect about the inner me or my spiritual garden?

My Present Priorities
- The most important thing in my life is:

- Other very important things are:

- Other responsibilities I have are:

Reflection: Are these my God-given priorities, as best as I know, or my own? How might God's differ from mine?

General Time Commitments
(For example: times with friends, hobbies, exercise, committee responsibilities, household tasks, and so forth)

Reflection: Over which commitments do I have control and can therefore adjust?

Specific Time Commitments

	Weekly	Monthly
Sunday		
Monday		
Tuesday		
Wednesday		
Thursday		
Friday		
Saturday		

Reflection: Does how I spend my time correspond with my priorities? If not, where are the differences?

Necessary Changes

	Weekly	Monthly
Sunday		
Monday		
Tuesday		
Wednesday		
Thursday		
Friday		
Saturday		

Reflection: How will I specifically implement desired changes? What can be eliminated from my schedule? What can be rearranged?

Obstacles to Overcome
- Practical/physical (such as telephone, kids):

- Emotional/spiritual (such as specific fears, guilt):

Potential Solutions
- Practical/physical:

- Emotional/spiritual:

My commitment to the Lord regarding pursuing a deeper relationship with Him:

Signed _____

Date _____

CHAPTER FOUR

Defeating Satan and Surviving Trials Through Christ

"Those along the path are the ones who hear, and then the devil comes and takes away the word from their hearts."

–Luke 8:12

"Others, like seed sown on rocky places, hear the word and at once receive it with joy. But since they have no root, they last only a short time. When trouble or persecution comes because of the word, they quickly fall away."

–Mark 4:16-17

Many forces work against a seed once it is sown. Left unchallenged, these forces can prevent a seed from taking root or stunt growth even if roots begin to form. Many seeds are carried off by birds or the wind almost as soon as they touch the ground. At times seedlings spring up on rocks, but the plants are scorched by the sun because there isn't enough soil to establish healthy roots. Jesus used these lessons from nature to teach spiritual parallels.

To warn and strengthen His disciples (including us) for the trials He knew they would face, Jesus identified and warned about various threats to the seeds He sows in us. He did this out of His love for us to alert us to dangers we may face spiritually. In this chapter we will look at the first two of five specific threats.

Examination of God's Word
Take a few moments to read the Parable of the Sower in Luke 8:4-8 and 11-15. Especially note verses 5,12 and 6,13.

Threat #1: The Devil

1. In what ways is the Devil like the birds who snatch away the farmer's seed?

2. What image do you think people have of the Devil today? How would you describe him?

3. How is he described in the Scriptures listed below?

    a. John 8:43-44

    b. Ephesians 6:10-12

    c. 1 Peter 5:8-9

    d. Revelation 12:7-9; 20:10

4. In what ways do the truths in these verses impact your view of Satan?

5.   Realizing there is a real Enemy prowling around (1 Peter 5:8-9), what message do these verses communicate regarding being alert to his tactics and schemes? Can you think of any parallels that can be drawn from military strategy during war?

6.   According to verses listed below, what power does Christ have over the Enemy?

a. Mark 1:21-27,39; 3:11

b. Colossians 2:15

c. 1 John 3:8

7.   Read Luke 10:18-20 and 1 John 4:4. What assurances are we given regarding Satan and his demons in these verses? How do these truths impact you?

God knows the seriousness of the ongoing battle against evil in this life, and He is very aware of our human frailties. Therefore, He has not left us unequipped. A detailed listing of our battle gear is given in Ephesians 6:10-18.

8. According to Ephesians 6:10-11, what two things are we supposed to do in preparation for spiritual battle?

9. Fill in the following chart by naming each piece of equipment of our armor, telling how it can be used effectively, and describing it as an offensive or defensive weapon.

Type of Equipment	Intended Use	Offensive or Defensive?

10. According to 2 Corinthians 10:3-5, how are these weapons described? (Especially note the intended use mentioned in verse 4.)

BETWEEN YOU AND ME
Strongholds can be defined as fortified or barricaded areas of hardness in one's attitudes, thinking, character, or spiritual nature. The Lord calls us and equips us to demolish these strongholds that

Satan has established in people's lives to prevent them from responding to the Lord in obedience or growing in Him (2 Corinthians 10:4).

The dictionary describes a stronghold as a "fortress." This applies to our lives in spiritual terms as Satan gaining a "foothold" (Ephesians 4:26-27). This can occur through a variety of avenues such as anger, fear, or rebellion. Any attitude or activity that allows even a small crack for Satan's penetration can lead to a stronghold. However, praying individually and/or with other Christians in the name of Jesus that a stronghold be demolished has powerful results.

For example, a Christian friend's husband (also a believer) could not understand the problem his new wife was having responding to him sexually. The intimacy of marriage caused an experience of sexual abuse she had suffered as a child to surface. He was neither patient nor compassionate with her. He even refused to go with her to counseling in order to gain understanding. His resistance was so strong that he began talking of divorce.

Several of us had been praying for some time for his stubborn attitude, but to no avail. Then we received the insight that there was a stronghold preventing him from seeing his wife's hurt and keeping him from comprehending. It didn't matter that we didn't know *what* that stronghold was (willfulness or simply a resistant spirit), but recognizing there was a stronghold, we prayed that it be demolished in the name of Jesus. As we continued in prayer over the next few weeks, his eyes were suddenly opened and he was able to see things from his wife's perspective. He was grieved over his former attitude and had renewed compassion for his wife. Their marriage was saved and is still growing today.

11. According to 2 Corinthians 11:14, how does Satan sometimes disguise himself? Knowing this can help us guard against his deception.

In addition to attempting to defeat or discourage us in our faith, the Evil One wants to create distance in our relationship with the Lord by luring us into sin. He knows how susceptible to falsehood and temptation we are. Regardless of the temptation, we can withstand it through Christ.

12. Prayerfully read 1 Corinthians 10:13 and then record what you learn about the following.

    a. The nature of temptation

    b. God's promise regarding temptation

13. According to James 4:7-8, what is our best defense against Satan?

Threat #2: Trouble Because of the Word

14. How does Luke describe the second threat to the seed in Luke 8:6,13? Why do these trials come?

15. Throughout Scripture there are accounts of the disciples and early Christians being persecuted because of their faith. For one example, see 1 Thessalonians 2:1–3:5. How can knowing about other believers' trials and being forewarned help us?

16. How can trials in general discourage us in our faith? What has your personal experience been in this area?

17. Read each of the following verses to discover God's promises to you during times of trial. Record those promises below.

   a. Isaiah 43:1-5

   b. Isaiah 63:9

   c. Romans 8:38-39

   d. Hebrews 13:5

BETWEEN YOU AND ME

As I have experienced many trials and difficulties, the greatest assurance I have found in the midst of pain or confusion is that the sovereign living God is with me. Early in my walk with the Lord, I focused on how things looked or how I felt, letting those variables determine my faith. That led to fear and discouragement. One example of this was when my parents planned to move to Colorado Springs from another state. My father was coming to stay with us while looking for a home near us only a few months after my husband had suffered a major heart attack. Because he was a difficult man, I found myself becoming anxious and over-whelmed with fear. It looked as though the Lord wasn't in control! I worried the dynamics would be harmful.

As I sought the Lord in it, He encouraged me through His Word. One Scripture He gave me was Jeremiah 42:11: "Do not be afraid of him, declares the LORD, for I am with you." That quieted me. I focused once again on who God is and the truth that He is with me. I stood against how the Enemy was using the circumstances to create fear in me. I also recalled Philippians 4:13, "I can do everything through him who gives me strength." My responsibility was to stay close to Christ and draw on His resources. Through it all, of course, I did find God faithful! How I praise Him for that!

Although I may not know what He will do, I know who He is. His promises to be with me and never forsake me enable me to trust even when I may not understand. Now every time I am tempted to focus on circumstances and feel that God is not helping, I remind myself of who God is and the truth that He is with me. When I get my focus back on those absolute truths, I again have hope.

18. In addition to His continual presence, what does God promise in Romans 8:26-27?

19. Because the Spirit of Christ lives in us and prays for us, what hope is ours regardless of our circumstances, according to the verses listed below?

a. Romans 8:28

b. Romans 8:37

20. Understanding some of the ways in which the Lord uses all circumstances in our lives for good can help us persevere through trials. This concept will be explored in depth in chapter 7. For encouragement right now, what benefits do you discover from the passages below?

    a. James 1:2-4

    b. 1 Peter 1:3-7

    c. 1 Peter 2:18-21

As believers we experience many trials simply because we live in a fallen world. Therefore we should not be caught off guard or be defeated by the everyday difficulties we face (1 Peter 4:12).

21. In addition to our present trials, what does Jesus say Christians will experience in the end times in Luke 21:12-19? What are we instructed to do in verses 14 and 15?

22. List specific ways Christians are experiencing persecution today, both as the church and individually. Consider also how this can be not only from society in general but also professionally and relationally (such as in a marriage relationship or with an employer).

23. What encouragement does Jesus give in Matthew 5:10-12 to help His followers endure persecution or opposition?

Reflection and Application

24. What new insights do you now have concerning the realities of Satan and spiritual warfare? How will this information impact your thinking and your actions?

25. How can the opinions or image the world has of the Devil be damaging to believers, especially new Christians?

26. In 1 Peter 5:8-9, Satan is portrayed as being on the offensive, trying to defeat us in our faith or distance us from the Lord. In what specific ways does Satan most commonly attack you? For insight, consider what is most apt to discourage you in your faith, immobilize you through fear, render you ineffective, or keep you from spending time in God's Word. Become familiar with your areas of vulnerability, because this is where the Enemy focuses.

27. For ways to combat Satan, review questions 8 through 10 in this chapter. Where do you have cracks in your armor? What equipment do you need to put on or know more about?

28. In what ways have you experienced the Lord's faithfulness when Satan has been tempting you? What are your responsibilities in resisting temptation? Be specific.

29. If there is a matter about which you have been praying for a length of time with no observable results, seek discernment from the Lord regarding a possible stronghold. Write down what the Lord reveals to you.

30. Ask God to demolish any stronghold Satan continues to maintain. If results aren't quickly seen, persevere in prayer and enlist others to join you.

In *My Utmost for His Highest*, Oswald Chambers writes, "The typical view of the Christian life is that it means being delivered from all adversity. But it actually means being delivered *in* adversity."[1]

31. What do you think Chambers means? Why do you think Christians often are surprised when difficulty comes?

32. Review these Scriptures that you read in question 17. Select one to personalize by writing it below in your own words and using your name as appropriate. Ask God to help you accept this verse as fact and to apply it to your circumstances today.

- Isaiah 43:1-5
- Isaiah 63:9
- Romans 8:38-39
- Hebrews 13:5

Between You and God

33. Are there situations over which you are currently agonizing and are not sure how to pray? Record them here and come to the Lord in your frustration and pain, being fully assured that His Spirit intercedes for you. Ask for insight regarding any strongholds that need to be demolished, or any other direction needed in prayer.

In conclusion, meditate on the truths in 2 Thessalonians 1:3-5, personalizing these verses as your own prayer.

CHAPTER FIVE

Letting Go of Life's Worries

"Other seed fell among thorns, which grew up and choked the plants. . . . The one who received the seed that fell among the thorns is the man who hears the word, but the worries of this life and the deceit-fulness of wealth choke it, making it unfruitful."

—Matthew 13:7,22

"Cast all your anxiety on him because he cares for you."

—1 Peter 5:7

Worry. It's one of our most insidious contemporary maladies. It can cause one to become physically sick and emotionally paralyzed. And it can choke one's faith. In fact, worry and faith cannot coexist.

God knows our propensity for worrying about the complexities and challenges of life. Therefore Jesus clearly warns us of this third threat to the seed of the gospel. But He doesn't stop there. He also provides care-ful instruction in how to avoid becoming defeated by it. This parasite does not need to thrive within, draining us of life and joy. In this chapter we will cover exciting and effective ways that worry and anxiety can be con-quered and replaced by Christ's peace.

Examination of God's Word
Throughout Scripture the Lord talks with us regarding the importance of what we focus on. Here again we learn a valuable and freeing lesson.

Threat #3: Worries of Life
1.   What are some common concerns people worry about?

2. Do you think worry is a symptom of a root problem or is it the actual problem? Explain your answer. If you think it is a symptom, what is the root problem?

3. Review Jesus' warning regarding the worries of life in Luke 8:7,14. In what ways can worry interfere with spiritual growth?

BETWEEN YOU AND ME

A popular song of the past was entitled, "Don't Worry, Be Happy." Wouldn't it be great if we could just stop worrying by being told to do so?

One day an acquaintance confided in me that she is a worrier even though her husband assures her it is unnecessary. She worries constantly about something—their children, finances, health, jobs. When her husband would tell her not to worry, she would put her anxieties aside for a while, but soon she would begin worrying again. Because there was no real foundation for her not to worry (that she was aware of), all she could do was stuff her anxious thoughts deep inside. When pressure built, her worries resurfaced.

No matter how much we may want not to worry, only truth can set us free. There must be a good reason to convince us we don't need to worry. In other words, some new fact must replace the perception that causes us worry.

Think of a small child who usually goes to bed without any fuss or worry. But one night she hears a noise outside her window. And to make things worse, she sees a huge shadow moving across her ceiling. Her parents can tell her over and over not to be afraid, or they can take her to the window and show her that the noise is just a branch of a nearby tree bumping the house and the shadow is caused by clouds moving in front of the full moon. With this explanation and proof, the child can return to her bed reassured and peaceful. This same principle applies to our spiritual lives also. Based upon God's revealed truth, our worries can be put to rest.

4. Throughout God's Word there are many admonitions not to be afraid. Each one comes with a reason. Look up the verses listed below and record the primary reason we need not fear or worry.

    a. Deuteronomy 31:8

    b. Isaiah 43:1-2

5. What two truths about God are revealed in Psalm 9:10 that can help us avoid worry?

6. As we have already seen in this study, one of the best ways to get to know God is to spend time in His Word. What quality of God is revealed in each of the following pairs of verses?

    a. John 15:9; Ephesians 3:17-18

    b. Isaiah 54:10; Romans 8:38-39

    c. Psalm 34:8; John 10:11

d. Deuteronomy 32:4; Psalm 33:4

e. Job 42:2; Psalm 138:8

f. Psalm 57:10; 2 Timothy 2:13

g. Psalm 139:1-4; Isaiah 40:27-28

h. Isaiah 43:25; 1 John 1:9

i. Malachi 3:6; Hebrews 13:8

BETWEEN YOU AND ME

I am not one to easily accept something as truth — especially if life seems to contradict it. In fact, I'm a seeker who wrestles with God until I understand. Thankfully, I have found that He meets me in my doubts. After earnestly seeking and then finding, I've discovered that my faith becomes more firmly established on a strong foundation of His truth.

I've also found that if we deny our questions about God or bury our doubts about something in His Word, our faith is actually undermined. It is much like what can happen to houses overlooking the ocean in California. As each storm hits, some of the ground on which the house is built erodes away. Unless the foundation is reinforced, it becomes so weakened, the house eventually crashes down the hill.

Our spiritual foundation can be damaged by the anxieties of life if we are not honest with the Lord about even little nagging doubts. He knows the very real threat worry poses to our faith, and He knows the threat is even greater when we deny having any doubts or worries. Because He loves us and is all He says He is, He wants us to be worry free. We can do this only when we bring all of our concerns to Him (1 Peter 5:7).

7. Prayerfully read Matthew 14:25-33. What do you discover regarding the importance of our focus? How does our focus relate to our being freed from worry?

8. What remedy for worry does Paul give us in Philippians 4:6-7? Why do you think this method works?

Worry or anxiety can be a warning that we want our own way in a matter. Dr. Lloyd John Ogilvie adds another dimension to this issue in his book *Autobiography of God*. He writes, "Worry over an aspect of our lives is a sure sign we are trying to accomplish our plans with our own power."[1]

9. When we take matters into our own hands, what are we in essence saying to God?

10. When this occurs, what is important for us to remember?

11. In Luke 10:38-42, Jesus makes a profound statement revealing a key to being freed from worry.

   a. What does Jesus say about Martha in verse 41?

   b. For what does Jesus commend Mary in verse 42? In what ways is this the secret not only in overcoming worry, but to life itself?

   c. Why do you think this is the key to becoming freed from worry and anxiety?

12. Is this an oversimplification? What gives credence to Jesus' statement? Consider the following verses.

   a. John 14:6

   b. Titus 1:2

13. In Matthew 6:25-34, Jesus again uses lessons from nature to reveal truths about God. What does He reveal as a key principle of God's provision in verse 33?

14. How does this relate to what He later told Martha? (See question 11, part a.)

Reflection and Application

Worry can be a habit—even something we can think is a responsibility. Some of us feel guilty if we're not worrying about some problem. If we're honest, all of us have our own personal set of concerns.

15. a. What are some of the things you find yourself overly concerned or worried about? Think in terms of the "what ifs" of relationships, circumstances, or future events. What are the things, big or small, your thoughts continually return to without a sense of peace? List them below in the "Concern" column. (For example, your concern may be that your son is leaving for college.)

Concern	Bottom-Line Fear	Truth

b. Review your list and consider what it is that particularly causes you to worry about each item you have written down. Now write the reasons behind these worries in the "Bottom-Line Fear" column. (For example, if my son leaves for college, I will no longer have influence — or control — over what he does. I worry about the things he could do and what might happen to him.)

Jesus proclaims that the truth sets us free (John 8:32,36). Review the truths about God's character you recorded in question 6 on pages 53-54. For a strong foundation that frees you from worry, meditate on those qualities of the One who is always with you.

c. Now consider which specific truths about the Lord's nature set you free from being fearful or anxious about your specific worries. Record them in the "Truth" column. (For example, the truths that can set me free are: I can pray and rest in the truths that God is sovereign and He is in control. He will protect my son and if He allows something to happen, He will be with my child at that time. God has already determined how He can use it for good, and has made provision for the needs that will arise. There are no surprises to God! My children are really not "mine" — they are first and foremost His. He is their God, heavenly Father, and Good Shepherd. I can entrust them to Him, who is always with them even when I cannot be. (For scriptural support, see pages 53-54, 60.)

16. What steps do I need to take to apply these truths? (For example, be honest with the Lord about wanting my own will for my son's life more than His and process that with Him; yield my will to His and pray for His purposes to be fulfilled.)

17.   After giving each concern to the Lord, leave it with Him, keeping your focus on Him and who He is. Then rest in Him. A responsive heart is a trusting heart! What will result according to Isaiah 26:3?

BETWEEN YOU AND ME

For me, a key attribute of God is His sovereignty. Being completely confident that God is in total control of everything at all times has changed my life and helped to set me free from worry.

Some years back we were scheduled to travel to Haiti. Just before we were to leave, my mother was diagnosed with a brain tumor. So we cancelled our trip and I flew out to be with her while my husband, Terry, took care of our three sons. Thankfully, the tumor turned out to be benign, and after she improved I returned home.

When I arrived, Terry expressed that he was very tired and intended to rest for the weekend at our mountain cabin. For some unknown reason he changed his mind and stayed home. That same day he went for a walk, stopping at a convenience store for a drink. While there, he purchased an issue of *Runner's World* magazine to read at home while relaxing. Ordinary events, seemingly without significance.

During the night, Terry awoke feeling very sick, but refused to go to the hospital until he noticed his fingernails were purple. At that moment he recalled the article he had read in *Runner's World* earlier that day and instructed me to take him to the hospital. The article, "Symptoms of a Heart Attack," mentioned one symptom we had not been aware of: purple fingernails due to lack of oxygen.

At the hospital, Terry was told he was having a heart attack and had he waited two more hours, he would not have survived. We later realized that had he gone to the cabin, he would not have read the article, and even if he had realized he needed help, he would not have been able to call anyone because we had no phone at the cabin. Also, had we been in Haiti at that time, the technology needed for him to survive would not have been available.

While we were totally surprised by Terry's heart attack, God wasn't! In His sovereignty, He had gone before us to arrange circumstances according to His plan for our lives. And I discovered I could trust Him *regardless* of what the outcome had been.

There are three ways the truths of God's sovereignty have helped free me from worry:

- I am confident that He holds my life in His hands and that nothing can touch me (or those whom I love) without His permission. He will use our circumstances in accordance with His plans. (See Daniel 5:23; Proverbs 16:4; Genesis 50:20; Romans 8:28; and Ephesians 1:11.)
- I know that God has the power to fulfill His purposes for me. It's not up to me to accomplish His purposes, nor do I need to worry that something (or someone) will prevent Him from doing so. (See Job 42:2; Isaiah 46:9-11; and Jeremiah 32:26.)
- I am assured that He will order my days (and times and seasons) when I rely on Him. I don't need to worry about what needs to be done because He is awesomely involved (usually quietly, but sovereignly, behind the scenes) in all that goes on. (See Proverbs 20:24; Jeremiah 10:23; John 10:3-4; and 2 Samuel 22:31,33.)

18.   For further study on God's sovereignty, read the first six chapters of Daniel. Record below all the proclamations and dimensions of His sovereignty you discover.

Between You and God

19.   Meditate on Jesus' name, "Faithful and True" (Revelation 19:11-13). In specific ways, how do the truths communicated in this name free you from worry or fear? What steps will you take to keep these truths in mind and establish them in your heart?

CHAPTER SIX

Avoiding the Deceitfulness of Wealth and Life's Pleasures

"Still others, like seed sown among thorns, hear the word; but the worries of this life, the deceitfulness of wealth and the desire for other things come in and choke the word, making it unfruitful."

–Mark 4:18-19

"The seed that fell among thorns stands for those who hear, but as they go on their way they are choked by life's worries, riches and pleasures, and they do not mature."

–Luke 8:14

You've probably received Jesus' warnings so far without question. We are glad to be alerted to our Enemy so we can thwart his purposes. We're grateful for God's direction on how to be sustained through trials and persecution. And we are thrilled to know how to be truly freed from worry. But do Jesus' warnings here regarding "riches and pleasures" make us slightly uncomfortable? Does it feel more like Jesus is meddling rather than warning? All of us certainly have possessions and enjoy pleasurable activities. Is Jesus asking us to give these up? Or is there something more threatening He is warning us about?

Consider what we are faced with daily in our society. We are continually bombarded by advertisers telling us our lives won't be complete without this particular product or that new experience. If we are not careful, we can begin to believe these messages.

Jesus is very direct and tells it like it is. He doesn't want us to be deceived. He is aware of the dangers we will face in our faith, and because He cares for us, He wants us to be aware as well.

Examination of God's Word

Threat #4: Deceitfulness of Wealth

Is God simply a spoilsport, not wanting us to have the things that make us comfortable and give us pleasure? To discover the meaning and importance of Jesus' warning, let's examine the Scriptures further.

1. Note that Jesus warns against the "deceitfulness" of wealth. In what ways are riches deceitful? What messages do we receive from our culture about the value of great wealth?

2. Does Jesus' warning about riches in Mark 4:7,18-19 and Luke 8:7,14 mean that it is wrong to have wealth? Why or why not?

3. What do you discern about wealth and the things we enjoy because of it in the verses listed below?

    a. 1 Chronicles 29:12-16

    b. 2 Corinthians 9:11-15

    c. 1 Timothy 6:17-18

4. Based on the verses above and 1 Timothy 6:6-10, what is Jesus cautioning against? (See also Hebrews 13:5.)

5. What heart attitude and manner of living does the Lord desire for us when He abundantly provides for us materially?

Throughout Scripture, the Lord reveals that what matters most is not the outside of a person, but rather the inside. After examining the verses above, we perceive that there is a deeper issue involved in Jesus' warning than simply being wealthy.

6. What further insight does Jesus give into this warning in Luke 12:15-21?

Oswald Chambers states a basic spiritual principal regarding possessions as he addresses Jesus' directive to the rich young ruler to sell all (see Luke 18:18-24). Chambers writes: "The principle underlying [Jesus' directive] is that I must detach myself from everything I possess."[1]

7. Why is detachment an important dimension to the issue of possessions?

8. According to Jesus in Luke 12:32-34, what is a key issue in this matter of riches? Express it in your own words.

I have discovered that in detachment comes a real freedom and peace. In the mid-seventies there was a severe economic downturn in Colorado Springs, along with a gas moratorium. My husband is a builder, and this affected us greatly. We ended up needing to sell our home. At that time I became very anxious because I liked our home and where we lived. I wanted to hang on to it. Through the process of selling our house and finding another, however, I came to realize several truths that have changed my life.

For one, I found that the Lord had a good reason in His purposes for us to be in another location—and I saw it was good! I saw Him use the economic downturn to guide us. He withheld the provision of funds to fulfill His promise to guide and demonstrate His purposes for us. I discovered the wisdom of how He worked in our lives as I began to see the good He had planned. So I came to trust Him more fully.

Another discovery at that time, which I have seen documented many times since, is that the Lord will protect what He has for us—if we are to have something, He will see that it becomes ours or stays ours. The home He provided for us to move into back then was the right one for us at that time. It was the Lord who worked out seemingly impossible details, and in His love, delighted to give it to us. I saw that He had gone before us and had protected the house from being sold earlier. That freed me to trust Him for other homes in the future.

The home in which we now live is another wonderful example of that. When we sensed the Lord's direction to move, we came across a house that I believed was the one the Lord had for us. This was during a time of economic boom and houses were selling quickly. We were headed out of town for three weeks and couldn't pursue purchasing the house at that time. It was so freeing to commit it to the Lord, knowing He would protect it from selling if this truly was of Him. Not wanting to live anywhere unless it was in His will, I could go to California with no anxiety about the home. When we returned, much to the surprise of many, the house was still available—and it did become ours.

Detachment—desiring nothing but what the Lord has for us, holding all loosely, not wanting to grasp or hold on to a possession—has been a freeing realization. It enables us to receive with thanksgiving whatever the Lord chooses to give, and offer it back to Him for His purposes—for whatever time frame He knows is best.

The deeper we grow in Him, the less possessions and position mean. In addition to the Lord's delight in our enjoying what He gives or entrusts us with, He also desires for us to seek how He might choose to work through it to draw people to Himself. Our joy is not in what we have, but in the Lord Himself!

9. How much money or wealth must a person have before he or she needs to deal with the issue of where his or her treasure is?

A. W. Tozer wrote:

Things are for us not only what they are; they are what we hold them to be. Which is to say that our attitude towards things is likely in the long run to be more important than the things themselves. . . . The world is for all of us not only what it is; it is what we believe it to be. And a tremendous load of woe or weal rides on the soundness of our interpretation.

Going no further back than the times of the founding and early development of our country, we are able to see the wide gulf between our modern attitudes and those of our fathers. In the early days, when Christianity exercised a dominant influence over American thinking, men conceived the world to be a battleground. . . . How different today: The fact remains the same but the interpretation has changed completely. Men think of the world not as a battleground, but as a playground. We are not here to fight, we are here to frolic. We are not in a foreign land, we are at home.[2]

10. What are some reasons or motivations people have to pursue riches?

11. According to John 12:42-43, what might motivate some people to desire wealth and the things it can buy?

12. What perspective on wealth and personal ambition does Jesus give in Mark 8:34-38?

13. What do you think are the true riches of life? Reflect on 2 Corinthians 8:9.

My perspective on true riches was challenged during a trip to Haiti with my husband, where I witnessed desperately poor families living in one-room huts with dirt floors. As these believers left their homes to attend church, their faces were not downcast. Rather, their expressions overflowed with joy and love. Although they had virtually nothing of the material things of life, in their spirits they possessed everything! They praised and worshiped the Lord out of full and thankful hearts. Their obvious spiritual riches in the midst of stark poverty impacted me greatly. Upon returning to the United States, I couldn't help but question, *Where is the greater poverty—in Haiti or in the United States?*

Threat #5: Pleasures of This Life
As the Author of Life, Jesus teaches us about true life. As we are His beloved, He warns us to protect our hearts. He doesn't want temporal riches to capture our hearts, but longs for our hearts to be set on Him and the

riches He offers that far surpass the things we see. These riches don't rust or fade, but are of an eternal, lasting nature. Out of this love, He also warns of another subtle but potentially deadly snare—that of life's pleasures.

14. Based on contemporary advertising slogans, song lyrics, television programs, and talk shows, what are some of life's pleasures that people seek or even strive after?

15. What view of this world and its pleasures are Christians encouraged to have? (See 2 Corinthians 4:18, Colossians 3:1-3, Hebrews 10:33-34.)

16. What do you think Satan wants people to believe regarding this world, their happiness, and their self-worth? How does he sell his doctrine?

17. Three ways that Satan uses the world to influence man are identified in 1 John 2:15-17. List them here and give a specific example of each.

Tactic	Example

18. After examining the Scriptures thus far, summarize why riches and life's pleasures are valid threats to the seed of His life in us.

19. What exhortation are we given in Romans 12:1-2? What does this mean in relationship to our perspective of this world?

20. What does Jesus offer us, as He stated clearly in John 10:10?

21. What admonition does the Lord give us in Jeremiah 9:23-24?

22. In John 17:13 why does Jesus say He has told us these things?

23. As we nurture a responsive heart, we discover that real joy is not in *things* but in a *person*—the person of Jesus Christ! What true treasures and pleasures do you think result as we discover this joy?

Popular nineteenth century preacher Charles Spurgeon wrote: "This joy is full joy. . . . When we get to know the love of God for us, we become so full of delight that we do not need or want any more joy. The pleasures of this world lose all their former charm for us. When a man has eaten all he can eat, you may set whatever you like before him, but he has no appetite for it."[3]

24.   Regarding our worldly circumstances, what does Paul reveal in Philippians 4:11-13 as the secret to contentment in any situation? How can this become reality for you?

Reflection and Application

Each of us has but one life. The way in which we live it has eternal consequences. In Acts 20:24, Paul expresses his life's purpose: "I consider my life worth nothing to me, if only I may finish the race and complete the task the Lord Jesus has given me—the task of testifying to the gospel of God's grace."

Regarding your own life, are you running the race you believe God has for you, or have you gotten caught up in the world's race? Remember, it's a matter of the heart. What is your heart set upon first and foremost? The following questions will help you evaluate your personal course.

25.   What is the race God has called you to personally?

26.   In what ways does the desire for wealth and the things it can buy appeal to you to the point of tempting you to get off course?

27.   What roles, activities, or things contribute to your sense of who you are (to your identity)?

28. What are your main goals or things you desire to achieve in life?

29. In what ways, if any, are riches or life's pleasures hindering your relationship with the Lord? Is your heart becoming more resistant to the things of God or more responsive? Give this careful thought. Ask the Lord to reveal to you anything of this world that has become as a "lover" to you. Then talk with Him regarding your discoveries and struggles. Jot down what He reveals to you.

30. Who or what are the major influences on your values and priorities? How does each influence align with the principles you are learning about cultivating good soil?

31. Of the three ways Satan uses the world (examined in question 17), to which are you most susceptible? Why might this be? What truths about God's kingdom do you need to apply?

Between You and God
Ask the Lord what changes, if any, you need to make in terms of priorities and activities. If you find yourself struggling with what He reveals, honestly bring your struggles to Him. As you dialogue with Him, search His Word and spend time in prayer and meditation. Seek truth and His perspective on life. A responsive heart is a heart set free!

32. Read 1 Timothy 4:7-8. With the context of a race in mind, where does Paul advise us to put our energies and what value does he say this holds? Meditate on these claims.

CHAPTER SEVEN

Persevering Through the Storms

"But the seed on good soil stands for those with a noble and good heart, who hear the word, retain it, and by persevering produce a crop."

— Luke 8:15

"Let us run with perseverance the race marked out for us. Let us fix our eyes on Jesus . . . so that you will not grow weary and lose heart."

—Hebrews 12:1-3

Storms do occur. Strong winds, heavy rain, and hail can make life miserable for a time. Yet trees and plants with deep roots survive storms and can even grow stronger as a result.

This is also true in the spiritual realm. Storms will hit, and Christians are not exempt. If deeply rooted in Christ, we are well equipped to withstand the strongest of storms. Charles Spurgeon talked about this idea when he said, "Our Lord, in His infinite wisdom and superabundant love, sets so high a value on His people's faith that He will not screen them from those trials by which faith is strengthened. . . . You are a tree that never would have rooted so well if the wind had not rocked you to and fro, and made you take firm hold on the precious truths of the covenant of grace."[1]

However, during the storm there is great temptation to give up the faith rather than to grow deeper in the Lord. God knows this and gives us direction and encouragement in His Word so we can overcome this temptation.

Examination of God's Word

We have already seen that life is full of trials—some are related to persecution for one's faith and others are simply a product of living in a fallen world. Let's take a look at the latter.

Amidst the Storm

1. What questions can present themselves regarding the character of God when difficulties and tragedies confront us? Which questions trouble you?

2. As problems arise we can choose how we will respond. Scan John 11:1-44 for a glimpse at how Mary and Martha reacted when their brother Lazarus died. What choice did each initially make?

3. At first, it appeared as though Jesus were indifferent, or not going to respond to Mary and Martha's urgent message. Why do you think He did not go to them immediately?

4. Given Mary's initial choice, what might she have been feeling?

5. What facts are we given about Jesus' awareness of the situation?

    a. verse 3

    b. verses 11-15

6. Did Jesus' delay in responding have anything to do with how He felt about Mary, Martha, and Lazarus? (See verses 4-6.)

7. What was Jesus' response to Mary's initial choice? (See verses 28 and 30.) What does this reveal?

8. When Mary and Martha came to the Lord with their feelings and questions, what resulted? (See 11:21-27 and 11:32-44.)

9. What does Christ promise to those who genuinely seek Him, according to Luke 11:9-10?

10. What do you discover about God's purposes from John 11:4,40?

11. What do you learn about the following aspects of God's nature from Isaiah 40:25-31?

    a. God's character

    b. God's provision

God's Higher Purposes

12. Upon examination of the account of Lazarus's death, we see that the Lord was accomplishing a higher good rather than meeting the immediate need. This is a principle in our lives also. In relation to this, what does Jesus promise in these verses?

a. Ephesians 1:11

b. Philippians 1:6

13. What are some of the higher purposes He is working toward in us today, based on the verses below?

a. John 15:1-2

b. Philippians 3:8

c. Hebrews 12:10-11

d. 1 Peter 1:6-7

e. 1 Peter 4:1-2

f. 1 Peter 4:12-14

All of this relates to God's sovereignty, or providence. Because the word "providence" is not commonly used today, let's define it. Jerry Bridges, author and former vice president of The Navigators, does just that in his book *Trusting God Even When Life Hurts*.

[God's providence is] His constant care for and His absolute rule over all His creation for His own glory and the good of His people. . . . [The] twofold objective of God's providence [is] His own glory and the good of His people. . . . These two objectives are never antithetical; they are always in harmony with each other. God never pursues His glory at the expense of the good of His people, nor does He ever seek our good at the expense of His glory. He has designed His eternal purpose so that His glory and our good are inextricably bound together.[2]

14.   How can an understanding of God's providence help and encourage us during times of struggle?

BETWEEN YOU AND ME

In addition to times of difficult circumstances, believers can experience "spiritual darkness" or times when God seems very far away. David expressed his feelings during such a time in Psalm 69:1-3. In those times we need to hang on to what we know to be true and to persevere, for God is working to achieve His higher purposes.

There was a time like this in my personal journey, which I call "The Way of the Cross." It was a difficult time, a painful time, a dark time. The catalyst was confiding with a friend privately about some struggles I was having in a close relationship and then discovering she went public with my feelings. This resulted in a confrontation with someone who was very dear to me. In that discourse, I felt led by the Lord to state some personal beliefs strongly. It resulted in a major crisis in that relationship and others. During part of that experience I wrestled with everything I believed. I felt alone. Like Jesus, I cried out to the Lord, "My God, my God, why have you forsaken me?" (Psalm 22:1).

Even in the midst of this season, I knew that this was one of the most important times of my life. During it I learned critical truths about the complete death to self that Jesus desires in us in order to more fully draw us into union with Himself. In wrestling with doubts, I discovered truths of His character in profound and powerful ways that have more firmly strengthened and established me in my faith. The Lord led me into discoveries and did a deep work in me that I needed desperately and am so grateful for. I discovered what the prophet Isaiah described as the "treasures of darkness" (Isaiah 45:3). Now these treasures are invaluable to me.

As we persevere through the "way of the cross," God faithfully brings us out into resurrection living. During that time, we are not aware how He is accomplishing what He desires, for it's a quiet and deep work of His Spirit. But as we seek God in our trials and yield to Him so He can accomplish His purposes through them, we emerge closer to Him, knowing Him better, stronger in our faith, and more Spirit-filled—all by His grace. Such a responsive heart becomes a delighted heart!

Building Endurance
Because only those things that God allows can touch us, it is important to remember that we can choose our response to difficulty. Oswald Chambers poses an insightful question for us to ask in the midst of the battle: "When my strength runs dry and my vision is blinded, will I endure this trial of my faith victoriously or will I turn back in defeat?"[3]

15.   How could posing such a question to ourselves help during hard times?

When difficulty comes, the first essential step to take is that of discernment. We need to ask the Lord if what is threatening us is of Satan and is not to touch us at all. If this is true, then we need to stand against it, rebuking Satan in Jesus' name, binding the Enemy, and preventing him from carrying out his intents (Luke 10:19). Then we also need to ask if, whatever the source, God is going to allow it to touch us in order to work His higher purposes through it. When that is the case, we need to stand against the Enemy's intents in it (such as turning us from the Lord) and yield ourselves to the Lord for His good purposes of refining us or our faith (see Hebrews 12:10 and 1 Peter 1:6-7).

For such discernment, spending time with the Lord is critical. As we seek, He gives insight through a specific Scripture or gives understanding through prayer. As we grow we become increasingly sensitive to His Spirit. When an understanding is from Him it comes with authority and assurance. He opens our eyes to what is going on behind the scenes and then empowers us by His Spirit to take any action necessary.

16.   Review 1 Peter 5:8-11. What specific instruction are we given to help us withstand Satan's attacks?

17.   Perspective is also essential. Throughout His Word, God gives us many promises and truths that are helpful to recall when we are afraid. Record those found in the following verses.

a. 2 Chronicles 20:12,15

b. 2 Chronicles 32:7-8

c. 1 Peter 3:20-21

d. 1 John 4:4

In *Surprised by Suffering*, contemporary author and theologian R. C. Sproul expresses some helpful thoughts about the relationship between suffering and God's plan. He uses the account of Joseph being sold by his brothers into slavery in Genesis 37:12-28 as an example.

> [God] triumphs over [evil] and brings His glorious plan to pass through it. We remember the dreadful suffering of Joseph at the hands of his brothers. Yet because of their treachery, the plan of God for all of history was brought to pass. . . . Here we see God working through evil to effect salvation. It does not make the evil of Joseph's brothers any less evil. . . . But over all injustice, all pain, all suffering stands a sovereign God who works His plan of salvation *over, against,* and even *through* evil.[4]

18. One aspect of suffering that makes it so difficult to endure is not knowing *if* or *when* it will end. What do you learn about this from the following verses?

    a. Psalm 30:5,11-12

    b. Isaiah 28:23-25,28

19. Athletes are willing to train diligently for the hope of winning the prize. What are some spiritual rewards of perseverance that can motivate us?

    a. Luke 11:5-13

    b. Romans 5:3-5

    c. James 1:2-4,12

d. James 5:10-11

20. According to Hebrews 12:1-3, in what ways does Jesus set an example for how we should persevere?

21. What is Moses' example to us, as recorded in Hebrews 11:24-27?

22. How important it is to maintain a responsive heart at all times! By persevering in the faith, what result is proclaimed by Jesus in the parable we are studying in Luke 8:15? (We'll explore this result in depth in chapter 9.)

Reflection and Application

The Lord desires that you honestly express your feelings to Him. He already knows what you feel and why; and He cares and understands. As with Mary, He desires to meet you in your questions and minister to you in your pain. As you express your heart and ask your questions, it's important to stay in His Word (particularly in the Gospels). A responsive heart becomes an enriched heart!

23. List any difficult situations you are currently facing in which you need victory. What are your thoughts and heart cries related to these circumstances? Write your response without reserve.

24. In whatever difficulty you are experiencing at this time, actively stand against Satan and his evil intents in it. He will use whatever he can to distance you from or turn you against the Lord. We must be on the offensive in this battle. Ask God to take whatever you are now experiencing and use it to accomplish His good purposes.

25. During difficult times do you usually find it easier to struggle and question God or to rest in Him? Why do you think this is the case?

26. Are you confident of God's providence in your life and assured He is concerned for your eternal good? Why or why not?

27. How can being assured of these truths enable you to persevere in difficulty?

28. What circumstances and relationships (past or present) do these truths help you with today? Release these to the Lord for His purposes.

It is through the severity of winter, when all is cold and barren, that a tree's roots do their deepest growing. This is also true during times of a spiritual "winter" or darkness. As I shared earlier, in my most severe winter I did not see any signs of spring—no leaves, no blossoms, no fruit. All felt cold and appeared barren. I didn't feel any stirring of life within me. Yet I discovered later that truly God's life had been active in me and was forcing my roots deeper into Himself. I came out of that winter stronger in my faith, and in the spring and summer saw the Lord greatly increase the results in all He called me to do. It has been quite awesome and has resulted in much praise to Him within me.

Madame Guyon, a seventeenth-century French author, referred to a seemingly barren season of the soul. She noted:

> The effects of winter upon the vegetable world seem to me to present a lively and truthful image of this operation of God. As the season of cold and storms approaches, the trees gradually lose their leaves. . . . During the whole of winter the trees appear dead; they are not so in reality, but, on the contrary, are submitting to a process which preserves and strengthens them. [Winter] concentrates their strength upon the root so that new ones are pushed out and the old ones strengthened and nourished and forced deeper into the soil. . . . It is even during winter that the source and principle of its life is more firmly established. During the other seasons it employs the whole force of its sap in adorning and beautifying itself at the expense of its roots.[5]

29. a. How have you seen this principle true in your life? Do you plunge your roots deeper into the Lord during trials more so than in times of ease? If you have not grown through trials, what do you think attributed to that?

b. Does the metaphor of winter, with the promise of spring, help you persevere?

30.   How have you seen the Lord accomplish good, in you or in others, through past trials to bring glory to Himself?

Between You and God

Oswald Chambers reminds us of God's goodness in spite of how things appear. He writes, "There are times in the spiritual life when there is confusion . . . when your heavenly Father will appear . . . [as] an unkind friend, but remember He is not. . . . There are times when your Father will appear . . . as if He were callous and indifferent—but remember He is not."[6]

31.   In what ways are Chambers' thoughts helpful to you?

32.   Review your responses under the "Examination of God's Word" section in this chapter. Which truths impact you the most? Jot them down here and meditate on them as you "fix your eyes on Jesus, the author and perfecter of our faith" (Hebrews 12:2).

Personalize and pray Paul's prayer in 2 Thessalonians 3:5.

CHAPTER EIGHT

Bearing an Abundance of Fruit

"Others, like seed sown on good soil, hear the word, accept it, and produce a crop – thirty, sixty, or even a hundred times what was sown."

–Mark 4:20

"This is to my Father's glory, that you bear much fruit, showing yourselves to be my disciples."

–John 15:8

Maximum productivity is possible for *you*. Note that the Parable of the Sower concludes with the promise that as we persevere in life with Christ, we will produce a crop that is many times greater than what was sown. This is exciting!

As explored in previous chapters, we are able to choose what our life will be about—whether we will pursue the things of this life or the things of God's kingdom. It is so important to make a conscious decision regarding what our lives will be about. How we live does matter! (See Hebrews 4:13.) If we don't intentionalize this, it's easy to get swept along with the currents of life without realizing it, and in the end, we may wish we had lived differently. How sad that would be!

Just how easily we can be swept along with the crowd was illustrated for me once at a United States Air Force Academy football game. As my family and I moved from the crowded parking lot up the stairs to the stadium, we were busy talking and simply flowed with the crowd. We weren't paying attention to where we were entering until someone asked for our tickets. Suddenly we realized we were at the wrong gate! We had to consciously turn around, go against the crowd, and make our way to the gate desired. As I realized how easy it was to go with the flow, I was struck with this parallel to life. How important it is to consciously make our choices, and perhaps at times to go against the crowd, to make sure our life ends up exactly as we desire—and more importantly, as God desires.

The good news is that if we desire a meaningful and productive life that is pleasing to the Lord and of eternal value, we have every assurance and confidence that this will be so. A responsive heart results in a productive life! The Lord guarantees this throughout His Word.

Examination of God's Word

Jesus used many parables in His teaching. Read John 15:1-16, where He again uses a gardening parable to teach us about the Christian life.

1. According to John 15:16, what has Jesus commissioned us to do?

2. Based on this passage, do you think the results are ours to accomplish or God's responsibility?

3. What key element of producing a good crop does Jesus explain in John 15:4-8? How would you explain this in your own words?

4. What is important for us to do to maintain our relationship with Christ?

5. As we fulfill our part, what does Jesus promise will result?

   a. verse 5

b. verse 7

c. verse 11

6. Paul reveals an added dimension to the truths of being productive in Ephesians 2:10. What does he proclaim, and what is your response to this discovery?

7. In John 15:5, what profound truth does Jesus state regarding our ability to produce spiritual results ourselves?

8. How is this same truth expressed in 1 Corinthians 3:5-9?

9. Based on John 1:4 and 3:6, why would this be true?

10. In what ways does this truth give a sense of freedom or relief?

Jesus' analogy of the vine and the branches in John 15 communicates these truths vividly. Consider the illustration of an apple tree. A branch of this tree, no matter how hard it tries, cannot produce an apple, nor can it make blossoms appear and create a fragrance. All occurs naturally as the branch remains a part of the tree. Life courses through the tree and its branches—and blossoms, fruit, and fragrance result naturally. Reflect on these truths for your life.

11. Does the freedom we experience in not bearing the burden for results mean we have no responsibility? What is the difference between *being responsible in* a task and *bearing responsibility for* it?

12. What importance does this reality then place on maintaining a close and growing relationship with the Lord?

As we realize that God does not expect us to produce spiritual fruit as a result of our own effort, we are freed to rest in Him and be refreshed by Him. As we do so, He desires that we return the love He has so freely given.

13. How does Jesus express God's first and foremost desire in Matthew 22:37-38?

14. According to John 14:15 and 1 John 5:3, what is one way we can show Him our love?

15. As the Lord refers to Himself as our Husband (Isaiah 54:5; Hosea 2:16), what does He intend as a result of the marriage union? Consider Romans 7:4, where in the original, Paul's words "belong to" mean "married to." How does this illustration impact you in light of the truths of this chapter?

16. The writer of Hebrews 6:7 says, "Land that drinks in the rain often falling on it and that produces a crop useful to those for whom it is farmed receives the blessing of God." In what ways does this principle encourage you as you seek the Lord?

17. Again read John 15:1-2. What does the Lord do in the lives of those who are already producing fruit? What do you think this means on a practical level? What will result? How have you seen this illustrated in your garden (or in another's)? How does this encourage you for your life?

18. As the Lord shapes and molds us, what does He ask us to do according to the following verses?

    a. Romans 6:11-14,19

    b. Romans 12:1-2

    c. Hebrews 12:1

The more of ourselves we give to God, the more He blesses us in our relationship with Him. As we draw near to Him, He reveals more of Himself to us. A responsive heart becomes an enriched heart!

19. In 2 Timothy 2:20-21, Paul uses the analogy of household objects and their intended use. How does this relate to God's purposes for our lives?

20. How does all of this relate to the condition of the soil explored in previous chapters?

21. Before His crucifixion, Jesus explained what would be accomplished through His physical death. He then relates this to us spiritually. What important consideration for maximum productivity is Jesus speaking of in John 12:23-25?

22. What do you think it means to "die to self"?

The root of this matter lies with the will, which is where self is strongest and most tenacious. In her book *God Is Enough*, Hannah Whitall Smith gives a helpful explanation of dying to self:

> The object of God's dealings with an individual is that this "I" may be yielded up to Him and this central life abandoned to His control. . . . But let us not make a mistake here. I say we must "give up" our wills, but I do not mean we are to be left will-less. We are not to give up our wills and be left like limp nerveless

creatures, without any will at all. We are simply to substitute for our misdirected wills . . . the higher, divine, mature will of God.[1]

This is the goal of abiding—true oneness with God.

23.   If you struggle with yielding control of your life to the Lord, consider the truths about your life recorded in 1 Corinthians 6:19-20 and 2 Corinthians 5:14-15. What is your response to these discoveries?

24.   Carefully and prayerfully read Luke 22:39-44. Based on Jesus' example, what are we to do when there's a conflict between our will and God's?

BETWEEN YOU AND ME

Let me share some more about my journey of "The Way of the Cross." During that time I discovered that the Lord desires to bring us to a total death of self. He desires that we do nothing out of self-will but rather walk completely in Christ's will manifested within us. This, of course, is a lifelong process, gradually occurring as we spend time in His presence daily and each time we choose to submit to His will. This also occurs through difficulties when we want to escape, yet we stay yielded on the altar while He does a deep work within. The more of self that is purged, the more we are filled with Christ and the more our oneness with Him increases. His will actually becomes ours!

The end result is not weak living, but powerful walking in His Spirit daily. (This will be explored more in the next chapter.) As we allow Him to do this work in us, our inner peace is greater, our joy is deeper, and our productivity is multiplied.

25. Paul points to Jesus' example in 1 Peter 4:1-2. How does he state the centrality of this issue?

26. As Jesus yielded to the Father, what occurred, as Jesus explained in John 14:10?

27. How does Paul state this truth for us in Galatians 2:20?

When Hudson Taylor, founder of the China Inland Mission, discovered the depth of this truth, it changed his life. The results were noticed by his friend Mr. Judd as recorded below.

> He had been a toiling, burdened [Christian] before, with latterly not much rest of soul. It was resting in Jesus now, and letting Him do the work—which makes all the difference. Whenever he spoke in meetings after that, a new power seemed to flow from him, and in the practical things of life a new peace possessed him. Troubles did not worry him as before. He cast everything on God in a new way, and gave more time to prayer. . . . It was "the exchanged life" that had come to him—the life that is indeed "No longer I. . . ." There was no thought of imitation now. It was in blessed reality "Christ liveth in me."[2]

28. Reviewing our parable, as Christ's life freely flows through us, what will be the results? (Review Mark 4:8,20.)

29. As our lives become increasingly productive, what is important to remember, according to Paul in 2 Corinthians 4:7?

Reflection and Application

30. How would you sum up the concepts shared in this chapter?

31. Review your responses on the "Personal Evaluation" worksheet on page 36-38 in chapter 3. What progress toward overcoming hindrances to your spiritual growth and toward fulfilling your personal commitment to the Lord have you made?

32. What other issues are you now aware of due to this study? In what areas of your life do you sense God's pruning and purging?

33. As God reveals new areas where growth is needed, what feelings do you have? List them here.

34. We often think first in negative terms (areas in which we fall short). Yet there is a positive perspective to growth as well. What challenges you in the areas indicated in the verses below?

Verses	Area of Growth	Feelings in Response
Matthew 9:27-30; 21:21-22		
John 14:12; 15:8		
John 16:23-24; James 5:8		
Ephesians 3:16-19		

35. How do you feel when you reflect on the fact that "apart from [Christ] you can do nothing" (John 15:5)? Is this an offense to you? Why or why not?

36. According to Romans 12:1-2 we are continually to present ourselves to God as "living sacrifices." Which one of the following statements best represents your response to this exhortation?

□ For the most part, I consistently yield to God's will, and His work in me.

□ Although I sometimes have trouble yielding, I desire to do so.

□ I often struggle with the concept of yielding to God's will — I like to be in control.

This is all related to the concept of dying to self. Be honest with the Lord about your successes and failures in this area. Process with Him any struggles or questions you may have. If you need help, consider asking your pastor, a Bible study leader, or a more mature Christian for his or her insight and prayers.

BETWEEN YOU AND ME

Early in my Christian life I tried to make myself into the Christian I thought the Lord desired me to be. My intent was to please Him, but I erred in thinking this was mine to do for Him. (If I truly *could* do this, Jesus would not have needed to die!) The results of my efforts in this were twofold:

- The Christian life felt burdensome to me.
- Whenever I thought I was doing a good job, I felt pride in my accomplishment.

Many Christians approach the Christian life in this same way. If it were up to us to mold ourselves into model Christians, our faith would actually be nothing more than a religious form of behavior modification.

When the Lord showed me it was "not I, but Christ," my life was changed. I saw that the verb "lives" in Galatians 2:20 is active. This means the Person of Christ by His Spirit is actually *alive in me*. As Christ lives His life out through me, the Christian life becomes "easy" and I am set free from self-effort. Then there is also no room for pride — for whatever in me that glorifies God is all His doing.

I had also thought the results of my service for Him were up to me. This misperception created pressure in my life. Then He showed me that the same truth applies here. I discovered that as He *lives in* me, He also *works through* me to accomplish His purposes. He showed me from John 15:5 that I cannot do anything spiritual in and of myself. God's Spirit is the only One who can accomplish spiritual results (John 3:6; 15:4-5). The more of me He is able to fill with Himself, the more He is able to accomplish through me—all to His glory! This is why Jesus says, "My yoke is easy and my burden is light" (Matthew 11:28-30).

37. In addition to bringing us joy and satisfaction, what does having a productive life bring God according to John 15:8?

38. From Jeremiah 33:9, what does the Lord indicate He desires our lives to do? Are you surprised to discover what we can actually give the Lord?

39. In review, what reason does Jesus give for telling us all these things? (See John 15:11; 17:13.)

Between You and God
What has been your experience with living a productive Christian life? Have you been carrying the burden of changing yourself and accomplishing results by your own effort? How has that felt to you? Or have you found joy and freedom in staying yielded to God and seeing Him accomplish His purposes?

40. Prayerfully read Paul's prayer in 2 Thessalonians 1:11-12. If this represents the desire of your heart, personalize it and pray it back to God by writing it here.

CHAPTER NINE

Reaping the Harvest of a Responsive Heart

"A man reaps what He sows ... the one who sows to please the Spirit, from the Spirit will reap eternal life. Let us not become weary in doing good, for at the proper time we will reap a harvest if we do not give up."

–Galatians 6:7-9

"You have made known to me the path of life; you will fill me with joy in your presence, with eternal pleasures at your right hand."

–Psalm 16:11

As we discovered in chapter 8, simply knowing God's will is much different from knowing and doing His will. As you reflect on all you have learned from this study about God's design for your life, you may feel somewhat overwhelmed. As you think of integrating all these biblical truths into your already busy life, you may think, *How do I add anything else?* Hopefully you have seen progress throughout this study as you have applied God's truths along the way.

You may be wondering how to discern God's will beyond the basics. You wonder what the Lord has for you when there is so much to choose from. You have the desire to please Him and want to make the time, but you are uncertain how to do what you know you should do.

Fortunately, as we nurture a responsive heart to Him, the Lord promises to guide us and give us all we need to walk effectively with a sense of peace in our hearts, order in our days, and joy in our relationship with Him as we experience His love in deeper ways.

Examination of God's Word

It is important to remember that just as a vegetable or flower garden cannot bloom the day after it is planted, God's Word will not come to maturity in our lives overnight. The Christian life is a journey and it has seasons. Regardless of where you are along that road, God's principles are practical and always apply to our lives.

Peace in Our Hearts

1. Jesus knows the turmoil of the human heart apart from Him. What does He promise us in the following verses?

   a. John 14:27

   b. John 16:33

2. According to the verses above, where is this peace found?

3. As believers, how do we achieve this peace? Read the verses that follow for insight.

   a. Philippians 4:8

   b. Colossians 3:15

4. The more we know about God, the more truth we can apply to our daily living. What do you learn about God from the following Scriptures?

   a. Psalm 23:1-4

   b. Isaiah 48:17-18

   As we realize that God is who He says He is and does what He says He will do, peace begins to reign in our hearts. The prophet Isaiah expresses this truth in a song of praise to God saying, "You will keep in perfect peace him whose mind is steadfast, because he trusts in you" (Isaiah 26:3).

Order in Our Days
All of us want to avoid confusion and disorder in our lives. As a society we pay large sums to attend seminars and purchase planning binders that promise to get us organized. While these things may help to some extent, the key to order in our daily lives is seeking God and His plan for us. Jesus walked in peace with a sense of purpose. We too can walk in this same way through His Spirit.

5. What are we told in Jeremiah 10:23?

6. How is the choice we have in this expressed in Jeremiah 6:16-17?

7. In order to totally entrust our lives and days to Him, we need to be assured that He knows us well. How aware do you think the Lord is of every aspect of you and your life?

8. What do you discover about God's knowledge of you from these verses?

   a. Psalm 139:1-16

   b. John 10:14-15

   c. 1 Corinthians 13:12

9. As He knows you and loves you, what does Jesus say He does for you in John 10:3-4?

10. Based on God's Word and Jesus' example, we can be assured that He loves with a perfect love. According to 1 John 4:18, what is the result of this type of love?

BETWEEN YOU AND ME

As new Christians it is common to turn our *lives* over to Christ and then take back our *days*. This can occur for a variety of reasons, but the results are the same. We take control and as a result often lose our joy. As we make our lists of things we need to do and are committed to do, we can become driven to accomplish them all (or at least I can). When I do this, my stomach gets in knots and I feel uptight. Over the years I've learned that when this occurs it means I have retaken control. Once I recommit to *His* agenda, peace and joy return.

One of the most freeing, thrilling, and life-changing truths for me has been realizing and believing that God has specific plans for and will sovereignly order my seasons, my days, and my steps. God is a God of order, not of disorder (1 Corinthians 14:33).

11. Each of the following verses teaches us something about God's plans for us. What do you learn from each one?

a. Proverbs 20:24

b. Jeremiah 29:11

c. 1 Corinthians 3:5

d. Ephesians 2:10

In Psalm 8:3-4 David is awed by the fact that God—who created all things—cares about him. He writes, "What is man that you are mindful of him, the son of man that you care for him?" As tiny as each one of us is compared to the vastness of creation and God Himself, He is aware of every detail of our lives (Psalm 139:1-4). He has also determined, before we were born, the works He wants us to accomplish (Jeremiah 1:4-5; Ephesians 2:10). It is one thing to know God has my days planned, but it is another to discern that plan.

Once again, God gives us guidance in His Word (Psalm 119:105). Throughout this study we have looked at God's overall will for us as His people. This includes His plan of salvation through Christ, our sanctification as we abide in Him, and a productive life for His glory and our joy. Now let's briefly look at how He reveals His specific plan for us as individuals. (Because this is such a broad topic, we will be able to examine it only briefly here.)

12. One dimension to discerning God's specific will for our niche in His family is to understand how He has equipped each of us. Read 1 Corinthians 12:1,4-13,27. According to this passage, what does the Lord give each believer?

13. For what purpose does He do this?

14. In verses 14-26 what do you discover regarding your role in His body? How does this make you feel?

Knowing your spiritual gift(s) helps you narrow your options in terms of service within the church. This is another step toward peace and order. We have learned that the Lord has prepared specific tasks for us, and He faithfully equips us for those. Discovering our gift(s) helps us identify the areas of focus in which some of our tasks have been "assigned."

15.   Look again at Philippians 2:13—this time from the perspective
       of discerning God's will. What does this verse teach?

Between You and Me

As the Holy Spirit works within us, He guides us daily. Two ways
He does this can be described by the words *freedom* and *restraint*.
By prompting us from within, God leads us to do some things
and not to do others.

An example of how He guides us in our daily tasks through
the freedom and restraint of His Holy Spirit is seen in my "car
wash story." One day I had planned to take my dog to the vet, get
my car washed, and shop at the grocery store—in that order.
Through years of practice, I have found it helpful to give my agenda
to the Lord step-by-step throughout the day. As I approached the
car wash, I prayed, telling the Lord this was my plan and asking
if it was His. Immediately I felt restraint—a sense that I should
not get the car washed right then. So I asked again.

I explained to Him that my car was really in need of a wash
and it was right on my way to the store. Again, I felt restraint. So
I went directly to the grocery store. I pulled into the parking lot
just as a friend was leaving with her groceries, so I stopped to talk
with her. As we conversed she expressed her struggles and fears
for her family as they considered a job her husband was offered in
Haiti for the next few years. As we discussed how understandable
her struggles were, we focused on the truths of God's character and
His promises. We also considered ways to discern His leading. The
more we talked, the clearer God's direction became. That conver-
sation was a pivotal moment for her. Had I stopped at the car wash,
I would have missed her. God ordered our steps. As a result both
of us were filled with His praise, peace, and joy.

16. Listed below are scriptural examples of the Holy Spirit's freedom and restraint. For each passage listed, write down the situation, how the Spirit led, and the result of obedience.

   a. Acts 8:26-35

   b. Acts 16:6-10

To establish and maintain sensitivity to God's Spirit, prayer is essential. We need both extended times of prayer when we seek God from the depths of our hearts and quick calls for guidance or correction as we go through the day. As we seek His mind, it is helpful to recall God's promise of wisdom in James 1:5.

17. Of what was Paul confident according to his testimony in Acts 23:1?

18. Do you think this assurance could also be yours? Why or why not?

19. Read Psalm 138:8. If you desire God's purposes for your life and for each day, what can you count on?

Joy in Our Relationship with Him

According to the Westminster Catechism, "Man's chief end is to glorify God and to enjoy Him forever."[1] Too often this is the last thing we think of in our relationship with Him. When we are with Him, we often are asking of Him—then we rush from His presence to serve Him. Asking is certainly fine, for we are dependent upon Him. However, our relationship is not to be solely petition. Sadly, we often neglect simply enjoying Him.

King David knew the Lord intimately and followed Him with his whole heart (1 Kings 14:8). As a result, David enjoyed His relationship with the Lord.

20. According to Psalm 16:11 and Psalm 21:6, what is the source of David's joy?

21. In John 15:9-11, Jesus expresses His heart for us. What does He desire for us according to these verses?

There is a difference between having a relationship and enjoying fellowship. If we have opened our hearts to Jesus, we have a love relationship from which nothing can separate us (Romans 8:38-39). Yet some maintain simply a "casual acquaintance" while others nurture a deeper oneness. The better we know the Lord, the closer we grow to Him and the more richly we enjoy being with Him. In fact, *He* becomes our joy! A responsive heart is a joyous heart!

22. Since it is out of His love that Christ came and gave His life, it is a love relationship He longs to nurture with each of us. What do you discover of this love in Ephesians 3:16-19?

Brent Curtis and John Eldredge, authors of the book *The Sacred Romance*, write of this deeper love relationship with the Lord. They proclaim, "Intimacy with God [is what] we were created [for] and for this we were rescued from sin and death. . . . God has had us in mind since before the Foundations of the World. He loved us before the beginning of time, has come for us, and now calls us to journey toward him, with him, for the consummation of our love."[2]

23.   How is this desire expressed by Jesus as He pours out His heart in prayer to His Father before going to the cross in John 17:25-26?

Reflection and Application

24.   Review Isaiah 26:3. In what ways has this verse proven true in your life?

25.   At times when you do not feel peace, what attitudes or thoughts contribute to this lack of peace?

26.   As you have spent time with the Lord, how has He given you His peace? Give specific examples.

27. As we abide in Him and He in us, we walk with purpose. We are aware that all is in order, and we have His peace as we become increasingly sensitive to the leading of His Spirit within us. If you can recall a time when you realized, perhaps in retrospect, that the Lord directed your steps in one of these ways, record it here.

28. What specific situations are you concerned or burdened about because you do not know either what to do or how to fit them into your busy days? List each one here, yield it to the Lord, and ask Him to reveal to you what to do regarding each one. For example: Does He want you to become actively involved in the situation? (If so, is there an involvement you need to decline?) Or is He calling you to pray for that need? Or to be His instrument in helping another, whom He is raising up, become involved?

29. As you listed your concerns above, did you find it difficult to yield anything to the Lord? Perhaps you didn't even list some things that came to mind. What might be keeping you from letting go? Honestly express your heart to Him by writing your prayer here.

BETWEEN YOU AND ME

For some of us it may be difficult to develop close intimacy with God because of past hurts, lack of love, or even rejection from those who should love us. God has helped me in this area.

I have found the love of Christ to meet my deepest longings. As I was growing up, I didn't realize that I was loved by my parents. I don't remember being touched, held, or told that I was loved as a child. In fact, I remember vividly an incident when my brother, then five (he is twelve years younger than I), said, "Daddy, I love you." My father angrily rebuked him, saying, "Don't you ever use that word again." I share this only to illustrate that there was little awareness of love in our home (although later I realized my parents did love us—they just weren't demonstrative people).

Yet I am thankful for this, for it was this ache within me to be loved just as I am that God used to draw me to Christ! The Lord brought healing to me through His love, and He continues to draw me ever deeper into this love today! How I thank Him for this! I've found and truly believe that no human expressions of love, as wonderful as they can be, can truly satisfy our deepest needs. It is the love of Christ alone that thrills my soul, my heart, my whole being. As I am fulfilled by the love of Christ, I can love others with His love. Now *that* is exciting!

In *The Perfect Love,* author Ruth Myers captures the essence of God's love toward us. Reflect on the following excerpt from her book:

In one sense [God] has no needs. But in another sense He has love needs. He has longings. And we as His loved ones can fulfill His deep desire through our love and worship, our fellowship, our obedience. . . . Each of us can bring Him joy in ways no one else can. . . . Perhaps you easily remember that God has compassion for you and is willing to help you. Or you may think of God as taking care of our needs in a somewhat condescending way—after all, we're His creatures, so He does His duty toward us. But maybe you've overlooked how intense His feelings really are—how He desires you, how much He finds delight whenever you cultivate your love relationship with Him as one who belongs to Him.[3]

30.   What does it mean to you that the Lord longs to be with you in special times—that *He* has a responsive heart as well? That you actually bring Him joy? How does this affect your desire to spend time with Him?

Editor's note: If you want to learn more about intimacy with God and how to develop a closer walk with Him, consider the author's Bible study *At Jesus' Feet* for your next group or personal study.

Between You and God

31.   Review chapters 1 through 8, especially focusing on the "Reflection and Application" and "Between You and God" sections. As a testimony to God's faithfulness, complete the following sentences.

- God has taught me these key truths:

- He has brought the following areas of growth as I've applied each truth:

- My relationship with Him has been enriched in the following ways:

32.   Rewrite the following verses as your personal prayer to God.
- Romans 15:13

- Hebrews 13:20-21

God's Invitation to You

God Almighty, Elohim,
The Living God is He—
Existing before all time began,
And reigning through eternity.
Forming the world with His own hand
All creation sings His praise.
He forms each person out of love
And orders all our days.
O precious daughter, do you not know
His deep abiding love for thee?
He gave His life that you should live
And experience true security.
Daily He beckons you.
Have you heard His call today?
He's eager for your fellowship.
Oh, do not turn away.
Let Him put His arm around you,
Lay your head upon His breast.
Cast all your cares upon Him,
For He will give you rest.
You know Him first as Savior,
A Friend so kind and true.

Then daily He bids, "Draw closer,"
So He can manifest Himself to you.
Each day is an adventure
As you walk with Him as Lord.
You find Him faithful to His promises
And true to every word.
As you plumb the depths of His great love
You discover: You're His treasure!
And as you love Him in return
You reap His joy beyond all measure.
Lord we're humbled, Lord we're awed,
To know You in this way.
Jesus, with grateful hearts we offer
Ourselves to You this day.
Out of overflowing hearts of love
We long to tell Your story.
For we've glimpsed Your majesty
And long to bring You glory.
We love you, Jesus, we worship You!
Our hearts and lives we give.
All we have we offer You
For in Your love we live.

KM

Chapter One
1. Dr. Lloyd John Ogilvie, *The Autobiography of God* (Ventura, CA: Regal, 1979), p. 63.
2. *New International Dictionary of the Bible*, J. D. Douglas and Merrill C. Tenney, eds. (Grand Rapids, MI: Zondervan, 1967), p. 1068.
3. Andrew Murray, *The Inner Life* (New Kensington, PA: Whitaker House, 1984), pp. 84, 86.
4. Oswald Chambers, *My Utmost for His Highest* (Grand Rapids, MI: Discovery House, 1992), October 10.

Chapter Two
1. *The World Book Encyclopedia*, Vol. 8, "Gardening" (Chicago: World Book, 1980), p. 36.
2. *World Book*, p. 38.
3. *The Lion Book of Christian Classics*, Veronica Zundel, ed., (public domain), p. 39.

Chapter Three
1. Leroy Brownlow, *Gardens of the Heart* (Fort Worth, TX: Brownlow, 1992), p. 7.
2. Oswald Chambers, *My Utmost for His Highest* (Grand Rapids, MI: Discovery House, 1992), August 28.

Chapter Four
1. Oswald Chambers, *My Utmost for His Highest* (Grand Rapids, MI: Discovery House, 1992), August 2.

Chapter Five
1. Dr. Lloyd John Ogilvie, *The Autobiography of God* (Ventura, CA: Regal, 1979), p. 61.

Chapter Six
1. Oswald Chambers, *God's Workmanship* (Grand Rapids, MI: Oswald Chambers Publication Assoc. Ltd., used by permission of Discovery House, 1953), p. 105.
2. *The Best of A. W. Tozer, Book 1*, Warren Wiersbe, ed. (Grand Rapids, MI: Christian Publications, Inc., 1995), pp. 84-85.
3. Charles Spurgeon, *The Fullness of Joy* (New Kensington, PA: Whitaker House, 1997), p. 97.

Chapter Seven
1. Charles Spurgeon, *Morning and Evening* (Grand Rapids, MI: Zondervan, 1980), September 3 Evening.
2. Jerry Bridges, *Trusting God Even When Life Hurts* (Colorado Springs, CO: NavPress, 1988), pp. 25-26.
3. Oswald Chambers, *My Utmost for His Highest* (Grand Rapids, MI: Discovery House, 1992), August 29.
4. R. C. Sproul, *Surprised by Suffering* (Wheaton, IL: Tyndale House, 1988), pp. 49-50.
5. Madame Jeanne Guyon, *Song of the Bride* (Sargent, GA: The Seed Sowers Publishers), pp. 400-401.
6. Chambers, September 12.

Chapter Eight
1. Hannah Whitall Smith, *God Is Enough* (Grand Rapids, MI: Zondervan, 1986), p. 78.
2. Dr. and Mrs. Howard Taylor, *Hudson Taylor's Spiritual Secret* (public domain), p. 157.

Chapter Nine
1. *The Westminster Shorter Catechism*, The Shorter Catechism (Adopted 1729), authorized by the General Assembly of the Presbyterian Church in the U.S.A., 1894. Philadelphia, Board of Christian Education of the United Presbyterian Church in the United States of America, p. 4.
2. Brent Curtis and John Eldredge, *The Sacred Romance* (Nashville, TN: Nelson, 1997), p. 97.
3. Ruth Myers, *The Perfect Love* (Colorado Springs, CO: WaterBrook, 1998), pp. 26, 34.